WHAT NOT TO SAY TO YOUR WIFE

WHAT NOT TO SAY TO YOUR WIFE

JASON HAZELEY & NICO TATAROWICZ
ILLUSTRATED BY SARAH SUMERAY

Quercus

First published in Great Britain in 2020 by

Quercus Editions Ltd
Carmelite House
50 Victoria Embankment
London EC4Y 0DZ

An Hachette UK company

A CIP catalogue record for this book is available
from the British Library

HB ISBN 978 1 52941 151 5
Ebook ISBN 978 1 52941 152 2

10 9 8 7 6 5 4 3 2 1

Text designed and typeset by CC Book Production
Printed and bound in Great Britain by Clays Ltd, Elcograf S.p.A.

Jason Hazeley is a comedy writer, podcaster and musician who co-authored *The Ladybird Books for Grown-Ups* series and *Cunk on Everything*. He also co-authored *Instructions for the British People During the Emergency* with Nico Tatarowicz.

Nico Tatarowicz is a comedy writer, actor, podcaster and musician, who has worked on the BAFTA-award-winning *The Armstrong & Miller Show*, *Murder in Successville*, *Crackanory*, and *Very Important People*. He co-authored *Instructions for the British People During the Emergency* with Jason Hazeley.

Things you should NEVER
say to your wife
are marked with a

What Not to Say . . .

. . . When She Hasn't Looked Up from Her Phone for Three Hours

If I get in there, will you talk to me?

Have you finished Twitter yet?

Are you reading about phone addiction again?

Listen – why don't you do all your bootie calls during the day, then we can watch a movie at night?

I think it's time you started wearing a dopamine patch.

Say hello from me to everyone you've ever met.

Just to let you know: it's 2044 and I'm married to a supermodel.

Have you joined a *Black Mirror* re-enactment society?

. . . When She's Ill in Bed

Is this another pretend one?

Can you sign this? It's your new will.

I can't believe you've let this happen. Again.

(SNIFFING THE AIR) Have you been peeling eggs in here?

Not like you to lie around moaning.

Do you want me to bring the dishes up?

Don't be offended, but I've booked you into a Travelodge for tonight.

playback NORMAL/EQ 120 µS

Date FUNERAL PLAYLIST Noise Red._____ No._____

I hope that Something better comes along - Jim Henson
Another one bites the dust - Queen
Highway to hell - AC/DC
Stayin' alive - The Bee Gees
The Countdown theme tune (for Casket lowering)
Get on up - James Brown
Cold as ice - Foreigner
Get up, Stand up - Bob Marley
Celebration - Kool & The Gang
Friday - Rebecca Black

I'm just making a playlist up for your funeral.
Do you think something from *The Muppet Movie*
is a bit too upbeat?

Shall I put some make-up on you? Because I'll be honest with you: you don't look great.

I know it's never been your thing, so I'm going to take this opportunity to go clubbing.

Are you definitely going to be up here all night? Because Dan and Ian are coming round for a FIFA tournament.

Shall we put your bed in the garden? That mattress could do with some fresh air.

Just to let you know – I've set up my drum kit. And this time there's nothing you can do about it.

You know Ingrid from work? Her other half's ill in bed too, so the two of us are off to the cinema tonight.

Are you going to even try to get better?

Glad you're not here!

Look – I don't want me and the kids catching this, so we're going to Florida for a few weeks.

. . . When She's Dancing in the Kitchen

It's amazing how happy you are near biscuits.

Is it only people with no rhythm at this party or can anyone join in?

Is the underfloor heating up a bit high? You look like an Albanian circus bear.

Are you hearing the same music as me?

Careful, love – the chimney's loose.

Have you got a wasp up your jumper?

Oh, good – is it mating season?

Just a little tip: it's better to dance like nobody's watching when nobody's watching.

. . . In a Supermarket

Shall I go and warn the gin that you're here?

Look – neither of us knows what a kumquat is. They might not be safe.

So: za'atar, panko, chia seeds and moringa powder. Is this a dinner or an intergalactic space war?

Let's get you to the wine aisle. These grapes look frightened.

See if they've got any burnproof rice.

I wish you looked at me the way you look at those doughnuts.

Don't make me watch you choosing a shampoo. I'll get a migraine.

Reckon we could get a blue badge on account of your hangovers? We could park right next to the doors.

Buy an extra box of tissues – I've got something to tell you later.

I'm going to go on ahead and see if there's anyone worth flirting with on the tills.

. . . When She's Home an Hour Later than She Said She Would Be

Oh, it's you. Are you going to do your impression of a sober person?

It's so romantic of you not to hang around for the tequilas.

If this was a job, you'd have been fired a long time ago.

You're early. I'm usually pretending to be asleep when you get in.

For a very special treat, can I watch you make your drunk snack?

I think we might have to get you the Usborne book of *Telling The Time*.

Don't tell me – you helped an old fella cross the road 300 times.

You're back. Another dream dies.

Damn. I'd already started looking at wallpaper.

Your timekeeping's up there with your rational decision-making.

I'm going to miss this when we're not together any more.

. . . When She Pops into Cath Kidston

Oh no – are you down to your last hundred bags?

I'll wait out here. I haven't got my sunglasses with me.

Still trying to get a Cath Kidston black card?

You pop in there. I'll go and watch a couple of films.

I would come in, but I haven't taken my anti-smugness tablets.

Why have I got the feeling one day she's going to mobilise womankind?

Give my regards to the von Trapps.

If she ever uses her floral patterns for evil, we're done for.

Can't you see she's *destroying* you?

. . . When You Pick Her Up from the Airport

Good job you texted me. I'd completely forgotten you.

You landed, then? Oh well.

I may have hidden some long blonde hairs around the house, but it's nothing to worry about.

I hope you're not expecting sex, because I've had enough of that this week.

Nothing much has changed here. Apart from the locks.

Well, they say absence makes the heart grow fonder, so, since you're already packed, why don't you hop on another flight?

Where shall I drop you off? Your sister's?

I missed you so much. For the first half hour.

Guess what? I completed Pornhub while you were away.

Can't believe you got through, after all the stuff I told Interpol.

Well, my end-of-holiday blues are kicking in. How about you?

Don't feel you have to come with me.

Don't get excited – I'm not here to pick you up. I'm a minicab driver now.

I was going to write your name on one of those boards, but I can't remember it.

At least you haven't come home with a didgeridoo.

 I've bought you a coffee, because you've got shitloads of housework to do when you get in.

. . . When She's Had Her Legs Waxed

I knew it. I knew you had legs.

What have they done with the strips? Because we could do with a new draught excluder.

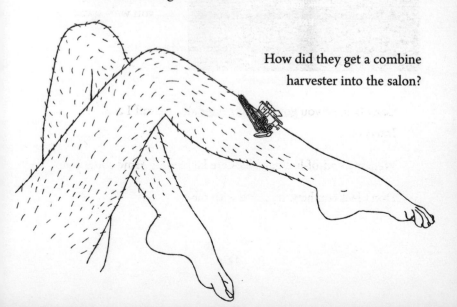

How did they get a combine harvester into the salon?

I wondered where all that static was coming from.

Think of the wigs.

Great. I was fed up sleeping in my shin pads.

Does that mean I have to start touching them again?

That's a relief. I thought you were transitioning into a Wookiee.

. . . When Her Best Friend Has Just Left

Now, listen – let her get to the bottom of the drive before you slag her off.

. . . While She's Following a Recipe

Would you like me to read out the words, darling?

Shall I book a few days off?

Have we still got that box of Diocalm?

. . . On Her Birthday

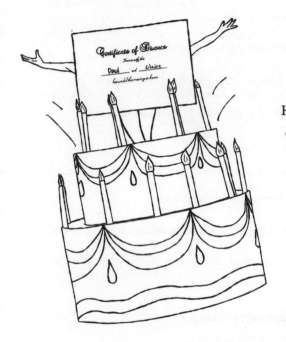

Happy birthday, darling – I wanted to get you your dream present, but it turns out I can't afford a divorce.

Now, don't get too excited, because I haven't bought you anything.

Nothing makes me happier than seeing your face light up, so I've borrowed this torch.

I want you to feel special – have you still got that plastic rose I bought you in Blackpool?

13

But I thought you liked salt.
And we always need it.

Roses are red,
violets are blue,
Here, have this
Because I didn't
know what else to
get you.
X

What do you mean, 'What is it?' It's a canoe.

I know you don't like me choosing you clothes, so I bought myself a shirt.

I went online to get you some saucy underwear, but I'm afraid I went down a bit of a wormhole.

Tell you what – let's do a deal: you keep lying about your age, I'll pretend I bought you a present.

What time's my sympathy shag this year?

. . . While She's Trying to Park the Car

There's nothing worse than some arsehole judging your parking, is there? Anyway, straighten up a bit.

You're gonna nail this one day.

Stop panicking and just PARK THE CAR.

Don't overthink it.

Listen – don't feel bad. Just remember: you're good at other things.

God, this is tense.

Don't shout, but you can go on courses to get better at this.

Try not to blink. Apparently it massively raises your chances of crashing.

What insurance have we got on this again?

You can see all these other cars, right? Just checking.

I don't know if I can handle this any more.

Wow, look how red you are. I'll take a picture.

Let's be honest, I'm the 'parking one' out of us, aren't I?

Shall we go somewhere more field-y?

Here's a thought: sponge cars. Just to save all this.

Don't panic, but there's loads of people watching you.

. . . On the First Day of a New Job

See you at lunchtime, then.

Just don't be yourself.

Just a little word of advice: don't talk to anyone there the way you talk to me. Because they might actually be listening.

Maybe save *some* of your opinions about the best Take That line-up for day two . . .

Did you change your name like I said?

Have you memorised the lies on your CV?

Be nice to the IT department. We don't want a repeat of 'Joshgate'.

If anyone's a twat to you, just laugh along – we need the money.

If you don't like it, don't worry – you can always go and work down a tin mine.

... When She Can't Find Her Bag

Maybe this is God's way of telling us that you don't need to go out any more.

Have you asked all your other bags if they've seen it?

It was full of rubbish, so maybe the bin men took it.

This is more tense than *Bake Off.*

Is this your way of saying you need a new handbag again?

Maybe now's not the time, but I just want you to know I'm really disappointed in you.

... When Her Parents Are Coming Over

Shall I put a bowl of wasps out for your mum?

... When You Arrive in Your Hotel Room Together

For fuck's sake. I told them to put twin beds in here.

. . . When She's Looking Absolutely Smoking in a Killer Outfit

Whatever I've done, I'm sorry.

God, you look good in polyester.

You look like a princess. Princess Anne. In her heyday, mind.

Have you been to the jumble sale without me?

That's good for £8.50, that.

Does this mean I have to dress up as Bill Clinton?

. . . When She's Entering Her Third Hour on the *Daily Mail* Sidebar

You've gone down the wormhole of hate, darling. Shall I throw you a ladder?

Is it well paid, freelance body-shaming?

You know you can just donate directly to the Nazi party . . .

You'd better come off there before you start talking like your uncle Alan.

You realise this is self-harm, don't you?

Have you handed in your feminism badge? Great. Fancy watching Miss World on YouTube?

Are you looking for ill-fitting bikini ideas again?

You doing that research job for Katie Hopkins?

Does this mean you're planning on 'stepping out to buy some milk whilst displaying your voluptuous curves in a daring mini-dress despite tough week' later on?

You do realise you're basically crowdfunding Richard Littlejohn's next skiing trip.

Let me guess: scientists have discovered a previously unknown Kardashian.

It must be terrible to have to spend so long doing something you're so angry about.

. . . When She's Running Her PowerPoint Presentation Past You

You might want to put some Lady Gaga on this so they stay awake.

Check out your design skills. It'll be missing-cat posters next.

Do me a favour: never, ever go on *The Apprentice*.

This'd better have a happy ending.

Is this what you do all day?

Well, now I know why you've never had an affair at work.

Remember: if they clap slowly, that's not a good sign.

Slow down a bit. Bit more. Bit slower. Actually, just stop.

This is going to ruffle a few feathers.

If you say 'going forward' one more time, I'm calling the police.

. . . In the Bedroom

I thought perhaps we could try some role play: do you fancy pretending to be my wife?

I know we said we'd leave fantasies unexplored, but do you think we could at least try a twosome?

. . . Halfway round IKEA

What do you want to do first – the meatballs or the seething?

I think you shouldn't come into the mirror section with that look on your face, in case they all smash.

Make sure you get another cactus you can forget about.

Open that wardrobe. Now, just for reference, *that* is what having nothing to wear looks like.

Look, you obviously love this bedroom. Why don't you just stay here?

Alright, Coco Chanel, you know we're in IKEA, don't you?

I like how far apart these two beds are.

This rack would be good for all your Gareth Gates and S Club CDs. It'd go nicely in the garage.

You should get another couple of cushions while you're here – make it a round hundred.

This is the longest walk you've had in years without having to carry your shoes.

You know these corner sofas? Could we get one that goes round a corner so we're not in the same room?

I can see by the look on your face that you thought we'd be shopping in Heal's by now.

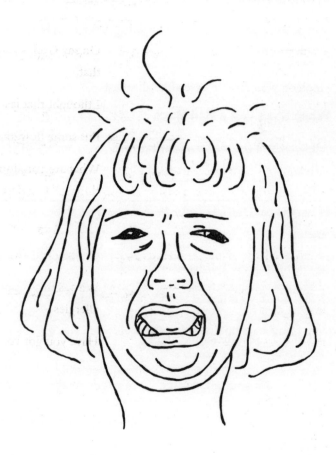

I'd never really thought through the possibility
that the kids would take after you.

. . . While She's Talking to an Elderly Neighbour

Sorry. She's been drinking all morning. Come on, love. Back inside.

. . . When She's Got a Bad Back

Have we still got the warranty for you?

. . . When She's Deliberately Watching that Programme She Hates

Is it time for your tutting exercises again?

Did she pull your hair at school or something?

Oh, I love watching your face light up when you really hate something.

Don't punish yourself, darling – you've got gossip magazines for that.

. . . When You're on the Ferry She Insisted You Take Instead of Going on Eurotunnel, Which Would Have Been Brilliant

So seeing as we're going cheap, does this mean we won't be going in any clothes shops when we get there?

Are you alright? You've gone the same colour as when I want to have sex with you.

Well, this is great. I love a prison ship that sells perfume.

I think we should do this more seldom.

At least on the *Titanic* we'd have some drama to look forward to.

I didn't expect it to be posh, but I didn't think the car park would be the nicest bit.

. . . First Thing in the Morning

Don't worry if you heard me say the name Vanessa in my sleep. It was a dream about a boat.

... While She's on the Toilet

If you're going to do that sort of thing, can you do it somewhere else?

What's that funny smell? Are you burning shoes in there?

Listen – don't panic, but they're evacuating the street.

Do you want me to stick a spoon under the door?

I've had a text from next door. They say can you keep it down a bit?

While you're in there, see if you can find where I've hidden the camera.

Do you want me to come in and show you where the toilet brush is?

As a courtesy, I've rung the sewage works and they've raised the threat level to Code Red.

Do I need to call a priest?

... At the Altar

So you weren't joking, then?

. . . While House-Hunting

This'd be a really good room for a Swedish au pair.

How much would it cost to get manacles on the walls of this kitchen?

I know it says it's an airing cupboard on the floor plan, but I reckon you could sulk in here.

Just out of interest, could we buy two separate flats for this much?

That cat flap will have to go. I don't want you sneaking out when I'm not looking.

And I think I'll have my *second* man-cave in here.

Now, I know you've always wanted a walk-in wardrobe. Hear me out: why don't we put a bed in here as well?

This garage should be big enough for all your skincare products.

. . . When She's in a Good Mood

You're in a good mood. How long have I got to live?

Promise me you haven't found God.

What's happened? Has Piers Morgan had a stroke?

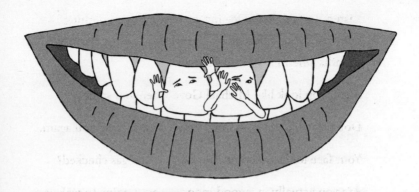

Be careful, smiling like that. Some of those teeth haven't seen daylight in years.

Let me guess: the Beckhams have separated.

Are you smiling, or is it just trapped wind?

I don't know who it is you're channelling at the moment, but tell them they can have your side of the bed.

You seem unusually happy. Do I need to check under the car before I turn the engine on?

You're in a good mood. Who is he?

Listen – while you're feeling chirpy, there's something I've got to tell you about where I've been going the past three months when I say I'm off to work.

Aaah. You look like Michael Gove when you smile.

Don't stay like this too long. I might start liking you again.

Your face looks different. Should I get the gas checked?

Are you actually in a good mood, or am I going to wake up in a minute?

Don't move. I'm going to go and get my camera.

Is this going to be like *Awakenings*? Are you going to go back to your normal self in a few weeks?

You know it's not twenty years ago, don't you?

Don't panic, but I think someone nicer than you might be trying to get through.

You're in a good mood. I'm just going to check all your stuff's still in the wardrobe.

Steady on. You don't want to sprain your cheeks.

. . . After She's Had Her Hair Done

OK. Let's not panic.

The bastards! Who did this? Did you get a look at them?

Jesus, what happened here?
Was there no mirror?

Let me guess . . . Vanessa Feltz?

Aww, you let a baby cut your hair!

How many haircuts is this supposed to be?

Whoever you're trying to look like, you look exactly like them.

It's going to cost a lot of money, but we can fix this.

You're leaving me, aren't you?

Oh look, you're twenty.

Whoever he is, he's not worth whatever that hairdo cost.

I always said you'd look good in a wig.

You should probably leave this sort of thing to Jennifer Aniston.

How much did that cost? You know I want a new bike.

Wow, you look young. Is it still appropriate for me to fancy you or do you want to drop me off at a police station?

Well, I don't know who this is for – you've spent your Going-Out Money now.

Are you getting your school photos done again?

Finally got the bollocks to join ABBA? Fair play.

That fringe is even more severe than your face.

That's a bit much. Did you shout at the hairdresser or something?

Stay there, I'll just take all the mirrors down.

☢ Babe, you didn't have to do this. I like you frumpy.

. . . Just before You Enter Your Parents' House with Her

I might have said some sex stuff to Mum. If she brings it up, just laugh.

. . . On the Morning of a Doctor's Appointment

Ask if there's anything they can do about your mind.

. . . At the Airport

Before you go for a wander, can I remind you about the mortgage?

Why don't you go and buy one of your celebrity colouring books for the beach?

Do you want to start telling me
how much you hate sand now, or shall
we wait till we get there?

. . . When She Phones You Up because the Car Has Broken Down

Well, what did you do to make it break down? It never breaks down for me. You must have done something.

Don't forget to lock it before you start walking.

You know I'm watching the snooker, don't you?

I'd offer to pick you up, but you've got the car. And you've broken it.

Yeah, yeah. Where have I heard that before?

How long do you think you can hold that thought for?

. . . When She Starts Taking Her Cupcakes Too Seriously

Please do not touch the artwork.

Are these for the Turner Prize?

When are you coming back? We miss you.

If you get this wrong, are we all going to die or something?

Well, these look worth getting angry about.

Oh good – I could do with a bit of heartburn.

Shall I take the batteries out of the smoke alarm?

Is this about Karen?

I see you've got your war face on again.

Are you rehearsing for *Dragons' Den*?

This'll show that smug cow at Monkey Music.

Before you get any ideas, I'm not running a market stall with you.

Is this a bad time to say those don't look very good?

. . . On Valentine's Day

You know what today is? Yep. Christian Eriksen's birthday. Don't look at me like that. He plays for Spurs.

There's a documentary on BBC Four tonight about Spaghetti Junction.

Don't think I've forgotten Valentine's Day – I've just forgotten how to have feelings.

Let's do something quiet tonight, like not speak to each other for three hours.

Don't buy me a new card – I haven't opened the one from last year yet.

I know you don't like big, romantic gestures, but I've wormed the dog.

Well, it didn't work last year, but here's your flowers.

Do you remember our first Valentine's Day? That curry was fucking sensational.

A bit awkward, this, but I'm double-booked tonight. Can you do Wednesday?

Let's go big tonight. I might not be here next year.

. . . While She's Putting Her Make-Up On

Keep going. You're getting there.

You know I know what's underneath this, right?

Have you got enough foundation there, or do you want me to nip to Homebase and get you some more mixed up?

Have you thought of drawing on an outline?

Careful now, love – one chin at a time.

Boy George! I've got all your records. How did you get in here?

Are you going to put some mascara on your nasal hair?

Tell you what, that looks lovely. Stay there – I'm going to get the Cuprinol so you can keep it on till next spring.

I'm not being funny, but if you want to get all that off before bed, you'd better start now.

. . . When It's Just the Two of You

Should have said, really, but I've written a will.

I can't stop thinking
about Eric Bristow.

Well, this is awkward, isn't it?

Shall we try facing away from each other?

I've got a good idea: why doesn't one of us go for a walk?

Strange. I used to enjoy this.

Shall we have one last shag and call it a draw?

Is there absolutely nobody we could get round?

I've written quite an angry poem. Do you want to hear it?

If you fancy it, I could probably saw this sofa in half in twenty minutes.

Just to let you know: we don't have to do this.

Hang on – I've just got to call anyone.

Sorry, love, I've booked this room.

I feel horny today.
Can we pretend
it's my birthday?

... When She's Making Christmas Dinner

Fair play to M&S, doing all this for you.

... When She's Hung-Over

Good morning, Oddbins.

It's not the antibiotics – it's the gin you put on top of them.

The hospital phoned – they asked if you wanted your stomach back.

If you're checking my face for signs of sympathy, you're still drunk.

Go and brush your teeth. It's like being breathed on by Scotland.

If you think you feel bad now, wait till you remember how rude you were to the paramedic.

Elizabeth Taylor's baton arrived for you this morning.

... When She Tries It On

Read the room, love.

Let me just complete this puzzle book first.

Where have *you* been for the last three years?

Is there a full moon?

I think you've accidentally taken some ecstasy.

Is it that time of the decade again?

You've been watching Channel 5, haven't you?

I'm not sure I can remember how to do this any more.

I thought we'd shredded the marriage vows.

Who sent you? Who do you work for?

Oh my God – your sex drive's been hacked.

Oh, that? No. That fell off about six months ago. I gave it to Oxfam.

. . . In Morrison's Car Park in the Rain

Is it raining in Morrison's car park? I hadn't noticed.

I haven't been this disappointed since our first date.

You really come alive here.

I've brought you here for a very special reason. We've run out of potatoes.

I never dreamed that this would be our life.

Listen – only a thought – but, if we stay here till midnight, we could try dogging.

This reminds me of that poem you read out at our wedding.

Kicking myself that I didn't ask you to marry me here.

Don't forget to say hello to your bottle bank.

. . . At the Wedding Reception

So, how long do you think we should stay married for?

Well, this is all a bit real.

I was only joking when I asked, but this is absolutely brilliant.

Shame about the dress.

Darling, this is my solicitor.

It's funny to think this is the best you'll ever look, isn't it?

Shall we just go home?

⚠ Might be a bit early for this, but I reckon Kelly the bridesmaid would be up for a threesome.

. . . When She Steps Out of a Fitting Room

Is there a sex fine if I get the answer wrong?

Remind me – is this for a fancy dress night or not?

I think that needs to be taken down a decade or two.

You didn't tell me you had an audition for *Loose Women*.

Alright, I'll tell you what I think of this if you tell me who should be the next England manager.

Let me see you without it again . . .

Wow. The new Doctor Who's a bit cocktail-y.

Tell you what – you'd give
Theresa May a run for her money.

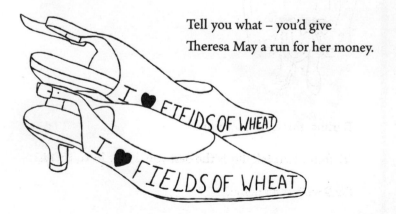

While you're at the shops, don't forget we're married.

I was thinking of kissing you when I get in, so start defrosting your face.

Morning. Didn't want to wake you, but I've moved to San Francisco.

you just looked straight through me at the lights

Stuck in traffic. Was trying to get away from you but I'll have to come back.

if you can hear knocking next door don't worry it's only me

Sorry who's this?

Just passed that Italian restaurant you like. It's shut down because we NEVER GO OUT.

I really appreciate everything you do for me.

Sorry that was meant for my therapist xxx

I'll Skype you when she's left for work WEAR THE THING

Hello. It's your live-in Ocado man here. What do you need today?

. . . When You're Introducing Her to Someone

This is my first wife.

This is someone I married.

. . . When She's Watching *George Clarke's Amazing Spaces* and Making Notes

Aww, it's lovely seeing you get excited about a new challenging idea for nine minutes.

Oh, this'll be good. This'll be like that time you didn't make any of those Christmas decorations Kirstie Allsopp showed you how to do.

Hey, don't go to all that trouble – just go and live somewhere else.

Seeing as this idea is going to go no further than that notebook, why don't you just try and get inside that?

While we're both drawing our dreams, fetch me a pencil. I must get this image of me and Scarlett Johansson in Barbados out of my head.

. . . When She Starts Growing Her Own Veg

You do realise you're about to spend eight months building a small salad, don't you?

Good for you, darling. Shall I do a press release for the slugs?

It's amazing. You can kill herbs quicker than Sainsbury's can sell them.

Is this the death-knell for that tin of peas we've had since the height of Britpop?

What's Mother Nature ever done to you?

I hope those courgettes have written a will.

OK, everyone – Emma tries to be Ruth Rogers, take seventy-five. Action!

Have you sold the kids or something?

If it's alright with you, I'm going to carry on going to the supermarket.

. . . When She's Training for a Marathon

Oh good. I've always wanted to see you on a stretcher in a tin foil cloak.

Why not destroy yourself doing fuck all instead? It's more fun.

Make sure you keep a note of all the sponsorship money you'll have to give back.

If you want to fuck your knees up, just keep eating brownies like they're grapes.

How are you going to do that? Are you borrowing somebody else's legs?

If you think I'm missing *Sunday Brunch* for this, you've got another think coming.

After you've done this, do you think you could train yourself to put your hair straighteners away?

I can sense you're nearly ready to give up, so I bought you these from the pound shop.

What's the charity? Prosecco Research?

If you think I'm pushing you around in a wheelchair, you can think again.

... On January 1st

You know that just wearing yoga pants isn't yoga, don't you?

Will it help this year's fitness regime if I strategically place Quality Street around the park?

Come on – you've given up sex. You can manage sugar as well.

I think 'regime' might be the wrong word. Shall we just say 'afternoon'?

Are you sure about giving up booze? You might give your liver a heart attack.

About this 'New You' – is she more patient?

Shall we change the locks so the Old You can't get back in?

. . . When She's in Hospital for a Routine Operation

I was going to buy you a puzzle book, but we don't want you getting a brain bleed as well.

I've written a eulogy for you, just in case. Do you want to hear it?

Do you know what? I actually prefer it on your side of the bed. Still, not long now.

I've had a word with your consultant, and you should probably swap that novel for a book of short stories.

Right – I've written a list. Which of this stuff is good to take to the charity shop?

Nice woman, that doctor. She reminds me of you ten years ago.

How are you sleeping in here? I mean, probably not as good as me . . .

Flowers are a bit girly for you, so I've bought you a tin of hot dogs and a strap wrench.

If I bring the ingredients for a bolognese in tomorrow, can you show me how it's done?

I'd forgotten how many women talk to me when I go out without you.

I bought you some grapes, but someone ate them in the car on the way over.

Well, I guess this is it.

. . . When She's Off to Book Group

I didn't know you could read.

And people actually listen to your opinions, do they?

Don't mention you thought *The Girl with the Dragon Tattoo* was well-directed, or they'll know you haven't read it.

Did you finish
The Very Hungry Caterpillar,
then?

Shame it's only one night a week. Could you join another six?

Don't do your reading face. You'll get drool all down your top.

Have you been hiding another brain?

You know Thomas Hardy's not the one from *Peaky Blinders,*
don't you?

Do they do colouring books?

You could take your copy of *Fifty Shades* once it dries out.

Are you OK? You look like you've been smiling.

. . . When You Call Her to See Why She's Still Not Back from the Chip Shop

Be honest with me: have you run off with a fisherman?

Do you want me to come down and read the menu out to you?

Ring back twice if you've got involved in a potato siege.

Don't rush back now – we've starved to death.

You know you didn't have to catch the fish yourself?

If you're not back in ten minutes, I'm going to eat your yoga mat.

Hey, listen: if you've not been served yet, come home – we've grown some potatoes.

... When She's Making Home-Made Christmas Cards

Don't send these, love, people will think you're not well.

Are they supposed to look like toddlers made them?

Oh look, a new wife. I've always wanted one of these.

Do we have to sign these 'Merry Christmas from the Swiss Family Robinson'?

Good idea, darling. I'll go and compose some carols.

Funny to think the person who made these is going to spend the next month in a onesie eating leftovers out of the fridge.

Is this you exacting your revenge on Paperchase?

 Someone's got time on their hands – is there no housework left?

... On Date Night

You again.

Right. I'm off for my date.

I was going to empty the
garage this weekend. See if
I can find your sex drive
anywhere.

. . . After She's Dented the Car

Oh, well done. You should get a matching one for the other
door next time you're out.

It's people like you that mean Chubby Brown still
sells tickets.

Did someone put a pillar in a stupid place again?

Well done. The patriarchy's going to love this.

Oh, good. I was wondering how we could get our insurance
up.

Does this mean you're not going to tut at my driving any more?

Did you drive off, like we said?

You do know that if I see a missing kid in the paper, I have to phone the police . . .

. . . When She's Sorting Some Stuff for the Charity Shop

Steady on, darling – I don't think they're that desperate.

Come on, love, getting some poor sod to dress like a twat isn't going to cure cancer, is it?

Exactly what kind of a charity is this?

Is it OK if I transfer my affections to whoever buys that top?

It's Oxfam, not the Strippers' Refuge.

. . . On Day One of Your Honeymoon

Good news – with the time difference, the match doesn't start until 9 p.m.

... About Other Women

We could ask your sister if she'd like to come swimming with us.

... When You See Her Internet Search History

You know those are not nice words, don't you?

I think it's time we made you a bunker.

Might be safer just to throw this off the back of a ferry.

You realise there's probably a desk dedicated to you at GCHQ...

Your Dark Web loyalty card must be nearly full.

Come on – it can't be that bad that you're thinking of joining Brides of ISIS. Just what they need: another martyr.

Is there anything in the shed I shouldn't allow to get warm?

Just be careful what hobby clubs you join.

Promise me you haven't left a manifesto on YouTube.

. . . While She's Buying Trainers

Remember how weak your ankles are.

I just want you to know that you don't have to be self-conscious about this. Loads of older women wear trainers now.

I kissed a girl who had a pair of those when I was nine.

It's so cute you still think you can carry *those* off.

These are nice. My mum wears these.

Is there anything racier? What about those glass-bottomed ones like they wear in mucky films?

Do you get a free adult nappy with these? Because you run like you've shat yourself.

. . . In an Expensive Restaurant

Two tables for one, please.

Choose anything you like and I'll find something cheaper.

I know you like us being modern, so I'm going to let you pay for this one.

Go ahead and have the Wagyu beef – you'll just have to get a Saturday job as well.

I'll ask the maître d' if he'll accept the Ford Focus as part-payment.

Have the scallops. Chantelle has them every time.

Yes, darling, it all goes with prosecco.

Just to be clear: I *am* doing this to get some sex.

. . . While She's Giving Birth to Your Child

I'll leave you to it. I'm going for a lie-down.

I know you're in pain, darling, and I've been there myself – I once got lemon juice in a paper-cut.

Do you think I'd suit leather jeans?

Hey, I've got something really funny to tell you after these contractions.

Most of these machines are German.

Come on. You're making a meal of it now.

Do you think Oasis will ever get back together?

. . . While She's Up a Ladder

I've looked everywhere for a job like this.

Will you be alright for a minute while I go and check the life insurance policy?

Those pants will be old enough to vote soon.

It's weird – I would have enjoyed this twenty years ago.

If you fall, can you get yourself to hospital? Because there's a pub quiz tonight.

. . . As She's Shopping for Holiday Clothes

While you're choosing a sarong, I'm going to start this encyclopedia.

. . . When You're Away for the Night

Will you tell your fancy man to fold my pyjamas before he leaves?

If you phone my room and someone else answers, it's just me doing an impression.

I've got a little surprise for you. Look in the cupboard under the stairs. I've put a new mop head on for you. Enjoy yourself.

I just thought I'd say hello while Svetlana's having a shower.

Got a nice view of the netball courts from here. Could you get my binoculars biked over?

I can't talk for long. There's a Bravissimo rep staying here who's got a knot in her shoulder.

Sorry I didn't call earlier. The red light district here is lovely.

Can we afford for me to live here?

Can you dig out the fax machine there? I'm just trying to send some divorce stuff from the business centre.

How are the batteries doing on that rabbit?

. . . When You're in a Pedalo

Have you ever read that book, *The Pedalo Murders*? I've read it fourteen times.

Shall we have all our rows for this year now, while the kids can't hear us?

Listen – are you going to be alright out here on your own?

Well, this is mainly me putting in the effort, as usual. Might explain why we've been going round in circles the last fifteen years.

This is like when you gave birth, but with the roles reversed.

Are you pedalling with your mind? Because your legs are doing naff all.

. . . In the Afterglow

That was a new personal best.

Do I have to be here for the next one?

Shall we say that one didn't count?

Where is it there's a shortage of Catholic priests?

A round of applause would have been nice.

I might get one of those Melinda Messenger pillowcases. No reason.

Well, someone didn't go to drama school.

Surely it's not supposed to be that difficult . . .

There's a damp patch on that ceiling.

Hang on a minute – we don't *want* any more kids. We don't have to do this any more!

Look, this is just getting a bit stale now – shall we try kayaking instead?

I'm sure this used to be fun.

This reminds me of the end of *Return of the Jedi*.

That's going to stay with me, that one. Just as well, really.

How many of these do you think we've got left? *As many as that?*

It's so much better when I don't have to pay for it.

Well, that was a nice surprise. Have you got your dates mixed up?

I could murder a plate of liver and onions now.

Might be worth giving ketamine a go.

We'll get there one day.

Ooh – I think there's a vacancy in The Saturdays.

. . . When She Joins an Art Class

When you've done your first portrait, can you have a go at the
skirting boards?

. . . When She Gets Back from Therapy

Whose fault was it this week?

My God – you're a different woman.

You didn't tie her up, did you?

. . . When She's Obviously Lost

Weird really – if I was driving, we'd be lost at this point, but
because you're driving, we're just 'nearly there'.

Don't worry, I'm pretty sure we're still in Britain.

I know you don't see eye to eye with the satnav lady, but she
has got a map of the entire world in her brain.

Right, I promise I won't point out that you're lost, if you
promise not to drive us off a cliff.

Who put all these French road signs up?

What's a non-aggressive way of telling someone they're doing it wrong?

I know you don't like admitting you're lost, so why don't we just go to wherever this is for the day?

You're getting some funny looks. Have you been lost here before?

Level with me – are you kidnapping me?

. . . When She's Dressed as a Cat Again for Halloween

See, this is how I hoped you'd dress for our wedding.

Does this mean you're going to start licking your thighs? Because I'm alright with that.

This explains why you keep wandering off when I'm talking to you.

Looks like we're going to need a bigger flap.

If you feel like torturing and maiming a defenceless creature and bringing it in the house, don't bother: you've already married me.

Are you going trick-or-treating or have you got a job at Spearmint Rhino?

Why do you always dress up so hot on Halloween? Is it because our sex life is dead?

Oh my God – you are going to scare so many mice dressed in that.

I thought that last one in the cat litter looked a bit big.

Put some flowers on your head and you'd look like a shit vase.

What are you doing? If we were dressing as our favourite things, I'd be dressed as *Match of the Day*.

Is Andrew Lloyd Webber adapting *Pretty Woman*?

Are you sure this is an appropriate way to dress to get sweets?

Who is this supposed to be scary for? People with cat allergies?

Have you got your three bras on?

. . . When She's Banging on about How Worried She Is about Her Sister's Marriage but Is Obviously Enjoying Watching It Fail

You were laughing about this in your sleep last night.

You should start a blog about this.

The main thing is: you've never let it get to you that you weren't one of her bridesmaids.

You know this isn't *Emmerdale*? You know this is real life?

Come to think of it, I don't think I've seen you this happy since you saw those Manolo Blahniks in Oxfam.

It's funny, sibling rivalry: you think it's deep within you, but actually it's all over your face.

Is this because at the wedding she made you sit next to that ginger undertaker from Stroud?

I'll say one thing: your sister might be better than you in nearly every single way, but you are winning at husbands.

Do you think you'll be this pleased when our marriage fails?

Is now a bad time to tell you I've always fancied her?

It's lovely how your skin glows when you talk about this.

You know the reason they're splitting up is because she wouldn't shut up about her sister's marriage failing?

Poor Venus. Did Serena thrash you again?

 Are they splitting up? I feel bad for sleeping with her now.

. . . When You're Passing a Massage Parlour

I wonder how old Babs Whiplash is getting on these days . . .

Reckon they do ice cream? Shall I pop in and see?

Your dad gave me some gift vouchers for there. I must use them.

To think, you were just a receptionist there when I first met you.

Have you ever thought about retraining?

Pull over a second – I think I left my AirPods in there.

How they keep their towels so fluffy, I'll never know.

. . . When She Drives past the Motorway Turn-Off

Oh, OK, tree-killer, let's go the long way.

Well, this is getting one star on Tripadvisor.

I'm sensing some deep self-loathing right now. Would that be about right?

. . . When She's Looking at Photos of Herself from Twenty Years Ago

That was that evening you smiled.

Well, it's not a time machine, but it'll have to do.

THAT'S what I saw in you!

I'm thinking of leaving you for this photograph.

Look away, darling. You'll only upset yourself.

It won't be long till you look like that again if you keep mainlining that kombucha.

How did I not notice that you were good-looking?

Gone to Stringfellows. See you in a couple of days.

I DON'T KNOW WHO YOU ARE BUT GET OUT OF MY HOUSE

IDEA: BE LESS OF A PAIN IN THE ARSE

GONE 'FISHING'

Gone on Tinder. Back in a few dayS.xxx
If an angry Pregnant woman Comes round, ignore her. She's mentalxxx
Your perSonal trainer phoned. He Says Stop it.xxx
SORRY ABOUT YOUR SELF-HELP BOOKS BUT I WAS OUT OF LOGS
IF YOU CAN'T FIND IT IT'S IN THE CHARITY SHOP

. . . As She's Unwrapping a Christmas Present

Don't worry, if you don't like it, Julie at work would really suit it.

Careful with it – I've got to take it back tomorrow.

Sorry if it's not what you want, but it was all they had at the Esso.

Now – believe it or not, I found this in a hedge.

I've given up trying to work out what you want, so I bought you this.

If you don't like what's in there, I can use them for Sunday league football.

Sorry it's a hand-me-down, but my ex looked great in it.

Careful with that paper – it's worth more than the present.

Now, this is more of a practical gift. It's that power drill you wanted me to have. Which saves you buying one extra present for me.

Before you open that, I want you to savour this moment, because it's going to be better than when you open it.

I'm going to level with you: I've not put any thought into this whatsoever.

I bought you one of these last year and you took it to the charity shop, so I thought I'd get you another one.

... When She's in a Bad Mood

Work's really stressing you out at the moment – why don't you go away for a few years?

Idea for a film: *The Lady Hulk*.

Well, at least we know your eyebrows still work.

We should bottle this atmosphere and sell it to the Taliban.

Looking forward to finding out what I've done to not deserve this.

Are you absolutely sure putting up with this was in the marriage vows?

This reminds why I had that panic attack before we got married.

Someone from the British Sign Language Association just texted to ask if you can keep it down a bit.

Why don't you go and have a lie-down in your ice palace?

Have you had a poo today? You know what you're like when you haven't done your potty . . .

Oh! You're in a bad mood! I thought a Siberian winter had moved in.

Cheer up, love, I feel like I'm stuck in a Stephen King novel.

Here, could I borrow your face to freeze these salmon fillets?

Can you make a bit more noise, please? I'm worried someone on the International Space Station doesn't know exactly what you think of me.

Phone the Met Office! Hurricane Shitmouth is here!

I'm just going to quietly go back in time and not marry you.

Hey – I've got a really zinging sexist response for this if you want to hear it.

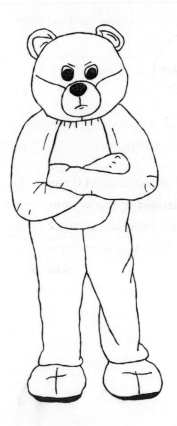

Could you at least wear a bear suit when you're in this mood so I have something cute to look at?

Keep it down, love – we don't want Relate's helicopter hovering over the house again.

Has anyone ever told you how hot you look when you're this mad?

Oh good. It's the *EastEnders* re-enactment society. I'll put the kettle on.

I'm glad you're in this mood, actually – I'd forgotten where every single one of my nerve endings are.

Oh look – a giant toddler. Would you like some turkey dinosaurs?

 Look, it's perfectly understandable that you're in this mood. After all, you are naturally oversensitive.

...When She's Upcycling a Cabinet

If you think you're giving up work to feel sorry for furniture, you've got another think coming.

While you're bringing things back to life, how about you have a go at our marriage?

Careful, love – I've heard this can lead to crocheting.

Ah, you're having your craft menopause.

Does this mean you're giving up wages?

God help whoever ends up sitting next to you
in the old people's home.

. . . On the Way to Parents' Evening

If you don't mind, I'm going to ask Mrs Jenkins what constitutes bad mothering.

. . . On Your Anniversary

Good news: I haven't forgotten our wedding anniversary. Bad news: that's your present.

. . . When She's Wearing a Face Pack

Bloody hell, that's got its work cut out.

I think I understand why pandas don't have sex now.

Does it work on stone faces?

Look at that. There's absolutely no smile marks on it at all.

Is that it, or is that just the undercoat?

Well, it's a start.

Could you be wearing one of these when I wake up in the morning? It's less harsh than what I usually get.

This is cool – I can't even tell what kind of bad mood you're in, wearing that.

Strange to think there's a princess in there.

You know I can see this, right?

Well, that's me not sleeping tonight.

How many more times are you going to try to invent time travel for your face?

I think we should invest in a Do Not Enter sign and some bats.

Come on, face mask, you can do it!

. . . When You're in the Wrong

This is horrible, being wrong. Now I know what you feel like the rest of the time.

Well, I look forward to hearing about this every fucking day for the rest of my life.

. . . When She's Trying Not to Sound like She Fancies Someone Who She's Now Mentioned Fifteen Times a Day for the Last Three Weeks

If I had a pound for every time you've mentioned them this week, we could afford a divorce.

Doing anything nice for your one-month anniversary?

How fascinating. Do, please, tell me less.

Are you being paid to advertise this person?

Oh good. This again. It's been nine minutes since the last nail in my heart.

Shall we get you a signed poster?

Shall I get you some new perfume or have they already bought you some?

It must be so hard for you two, being apart like this.

Do you want me to call you a taxi?

Oh dear, someone's ears must be burning. I do hope their whole head doesn't explode in flames.

. . . When She Suggests It's Time You Tried for a Baby

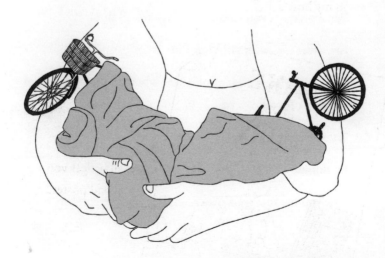

That's a great idea. Or . . .
we could just get two bikes.

Does it absolutely have to be mine?

That reminds me – we've been invited to a swingers' party.

. . . When a New Pair of Boots Appears in the Wardrobe

Shall I not see these yet, so you can say you've had them ages?

That bonfire you had last week – was it mainly receipts?

Well, they'll look nice in the pawnbroker's window.

These boots are made for walking – back to the fucking shop.

We should get you some more legs for all these shoes.

Are these for never going out in?

Remind me not to mention these when you say you've got nothing to wear.

Those would look nice still in the shop.

Be honest with me: have you killed one of Little Mix?

Can you file the heels down on these before you throw them at me?

. . . When She Suggests Renewing Your Wedding Vows

If we're going to do that, I'm going to renew my stag weekend first.

. . . On Holiday

This honestly couldn't be any more perfect. Except if I was on my own.

Does this mean you're going to be dressing like an extra from *Mamma Mia* for two weeks?

Why don't you swim out to the horizon?

Just remember – on the flight, the gin bottles are tiny for a reason.

I never thought it would be daytime drinking that saved our marriage.

Who are you going on holiday with next year?

Quick. Let's get a photo taken while we don't look like we hate each other.

I like you like this. You should get drunk and wear a bikini at home.

It's such a refreshing change to have you moaning about the heat instead of work.

God, I miss everyone else.

That tan really brings out the yellow in your teeth.

You smile so much more when you're on holiday. See if you can remember how to do it when we get home.

Don't try your French on that waiter again tonight. He looked like he was going to burst.

I'm looking forward to tasting your version of this when you find it in Asda.

Tell you what: it's a lot harder to ignore each other when there's no one else around.

I've heard the sharks round here are vegetarian. Why don't you go for a swim?

. . . In a Greetings Card

Nice to have met you.

I don't want to give you the wrong idea, so I'll just leave it at this.

I wrote you a poem. You'll find it scratched into the table.

I know you really go in for Valentine's Day, so I'd just like to say Happy Birthday for whenever that is (I can't remember) and Merry Christmas and I'm sorry for your loss xxx

I'm not good with words, so here's an outline of my cock and balls.

. . . When She's Off to Box Fit

Shall I pick you up in an ambulance, or do you want to call it yourself?

. . . At the Top of the Eiffel Tower

Unconventional place for a break-up, but here we go . . .

This is where I asked Emily to marry me. Wonder what she's doing now.

I thought I'd feel something up here, but . . . nothing.

There's something I've always wanted to say to you. That sound you make when you're chewing really gets on my tits.

Doesn't the financial district look beautiful?

You know this was only meant to be temporary, don't you? A bit like us.

Oh, darling, look! There's a bloke down there going through the bins.

Weird to think this'll be here long after we've both remarried.

I still say
Blackpool's
better.

I spy, with my little eye, something beginning with
the end of our relationship.

... While You're Going through Your Wedding Photographs

She was a *really* good bridesmaid, wasn't she?

It's funny – I don't remember any of this.

Christ. It's amazing what booze'll help you get through.

Actually, your hair doesn't look as bad as I remember.

Look at you. Gorgeous. You were the prettiest girl I'd ever kissed at that point.

Have we still got the receipt for all this?

I remember that day like it was yesterday. United lost 3–0 to Tottenham.

Wonder if that make-up girl has still got the blueprints . . .

There's your mum. I don't know what she was looking for in my pocket.

I can still remember when your dad went down on one knee and begged me to take you off his hands.

I was so tired that day. If it wasn't for the coke your nan gave me, I don't know if I'd have got through it.

Weird to think that flower girl's a stripper now.

Your dad said I'd grow to like you. Just shows you what he knows.

. . . While She's on the Phone

(MOUTHING SILENTLY) I'm leaving you.

. . . Ever

☢ Do you reckon we could split this house down the middle?

☢ Darling, have we still got those cyanide pills?

☢ I probably should have asked you this years ago, but is that your real voice?

☢ How do you want to play it if you end up in a wheelchair?

☢ I've got it. I know who you remind me of: gangrene.

☢ It says here that quite a lot of the time having an affair is *good* for the relationship.

☢ I was talking to a really interesting divorce lawyer the
other day.

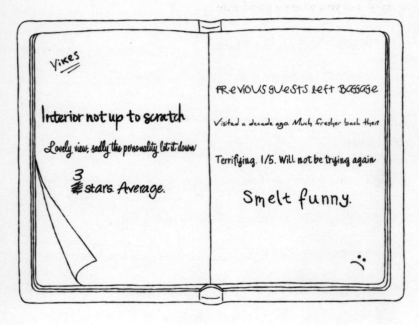

☢ Don't forget to sign my guestbook
before you leave this relationship.

☢ Right, well, that's my life done. What else can you ruin?

☢ I'm just nipping out to get my 'No Regrets' tattoo removed.

☢ Tell you who's a good wife . . .

If you have been offended by anything in this book, please fill in this complaints form and send it to the publisher directly.

I/we/they (delete as applicable) bought this book in the expectation that it would make me/us/them laugh.

However, when I/we/they read out some of the lines from it to my/our/their husband/wife/partner, they/they/they left me/us/them and ran off with a dentist/local councillor/labrador, and are now living happily in Toulouse/Cleethorpes/sin.

I/we/they demand that you apologise/refund me/unpublish this book immediately, or you will leave me/us/them no alternative but to seek legal advice/knock over your bins/go off-grid and become a cress farmer.

I/we/they look forward to your grovelling/legalistic/arsey reply.

Yours furiously,

Here is the reply you will receive.

Dear Sir/Madam/neither,

Thank you for submitting your complaint. We would kindly refer you to the title of the book.

Yours Sincerely,

Chief Replier

Department of Complaints

Hachette Books